Advance Praise

"*Meditation in a Ti*
the need to have tools to access that inner state that's similar to the 'Peace that Defies Understanding.' This peaceful or calmer state can be achieved while in the midst of turmoil, upheaval, loss, grief, threats to people of good conscience, families and communities of color, global threat, whether manmade or in balance in our ecosystems. From there we can think clearer and be more decisive about the appropriate necessary actions needed to shift us out of a state of manmade madness."

—Thaddeus Gamory, Police Lieutenant, NYPD (retired)

"Dr. Carol Penn is a calming spirit in a time of manufactured chaos. *Meditation in a Time of Madness* is not about being quiet, but rather how do we protect ourselves from the polluted mundane? It's a triumphant testimonial of the journey we must all take to self-love. While so many of us have been thrown overboard, washed ashore, and challenged by life's uncertainty, let Dr. Penn's rhythmic dance of words and wise guidance inspire us to be more than who we ever thought we were, in this moment."

—Gilda Rogers is the author of *Out of the Ashes Came Hope*, *Arrested Development: The State of Black Achievement and Education*, and *Fearless: A Bold Approach to Reinventing Your Life*

"I am grateful to Dr. Carol for providing these powerful tools and insights for the battle of our lives and more importantly the lives of our children. Dr. Carol is prompting the next generation forward to assume leadership of their minds, bodies, and spirits. As a parent and fellow warrior of spiritual awakening, BRAVO and Thank You."

—Diem Jones, Executive Director,
Voices of Our Nations Arts Foundation

"In today's time it is imperative to think logically with an aim to maneuver with agility, mindfulness, and distinction. Dr. Carol Penn affords you that very opportunity through her meditative tools. Allow her meditative guideposts to transform your subconsciousness. Engage your mind in order to find your peaceful place in a world of chaos."

—Dr. Afriyie Randle, DO, Physician

"A must read!!!! Very powerful tools for parents and children to incorporate in their daily lives. A must have for any family hoping to navigate in today's society without losing their direction and focus."

—K. DuBois, Educator and Caregiver

"Our world is in crisis and as an educator I see that on a daily basis. Kids are turned off and tuned into their electronic devices and it is not always easy to remain positive and hopeful in my profession. Ten days with Dr. Carol helped me to reset my mindset and my spirit. I am forever grateful to this warm and wonderful soul that I now have the privilege to call my friend. This book is important for all of those who wish to bring light into our world and help Carol on her mission. We collectively have the power to create change."

—Jill, A Blessed Lion Queen, Educator

"Dr. Carol empowers us to help and heal ourselves, teaching a holistic approach to self-care but utilizing ancient traditions including meditation, guided imagery, yoga, QiGong, and prayer."

—Rita S., Nurse and Parent

"A beautiful and well-intended book that will help so many people to deal with the turbulent and stressing times we are living today."

—Rosa D. Rabin, Musician, Composer, Meditation Teacher

MEDITATION IN A TIME OF MADNESS

MEDITATION IN A TIME OF MADNESS

A Guidebook for Talented Tweens, Teens, Their Parents and Guardians Who Need to Thrive

DR. CAROL PENN, DO, ABOM, FACOFP

MEDITATION IN A TIME OF MADNESS

Published by Publish Your Gift®
An imprint of Purposely Created Publishing Group, LLC

Printed in the United States of America

ISBN: 978-1-64484-414-4 (print)
ISBN: 978-1-64484-415-1 (ebook)

For Keita Omowale Erskine

I had a child because I wanted to know what it might be like to gaze into the eyes of God and, in you and through you, I came to know that unfathomable Love of the Beloved and the unwavering gaze of unconditional Love.

For Dima Afchi Jones

You also are a gift of Love, the gift that came when your father and I joined our families together in Marriage.

For both of you, I wish you Freedom, safe harbor, and safe passage in a world that needs to be blessed by your gifts.

For all of my cultural children of all colors and ethnicities, may you walk in your faith, hope, and dreams.

Table of Contents

Foreword

My sisterfriend and colleague, Dr. Carol Penn has written a book that is both timeless and timely and so important for families living in today's challenging times. In her preface, she writes, "I am writing this book because I do not want to feel helpless in front of some faceless enemy that seems to be both everywhere and nowhere all at once… I am writing this book because I will not give up my power so easily. I am writing this book because I am not helpless."

She is absolutely right. We are living in a moment driven by fear and ignorance, where truth has been trivialized, deemed meaningless, or worst still, irrelevant. Simultaneously, we are living in the "information age," with ceaseless streams of media alerts, tweets, Facebook likes, breaking news, and the ability to curate our own reality through technology. This is a culture fueled by disruption and distraction. It is one of the most powerful contradictions of our time: technology has given us the ability to connect with friends, family, business contacts the world over, yet so many of us experience an overwhelming sense of disconnection.

This is why *Meditation in a Time of Madness* is essential reading for you and your family. In her book, Dr. Penn teaches "evidence-based practices from globally proven wisdom and healing traditions." Her topics include meditation, guided imagery, yoga, qigong, prayer and spiritual development. These are all tools that I personally use and that we share with the WURD Radio family and community. And what I know for sure is that cultivating a sense of mindfulness to harness the power of our mind and heart is absolutely essential. As a parent, businesswoman, community leader and activist, I believe the time for this important book is now and belongs in the home of children from all nations facing the challenges of today.

Sara Lomax-Reese
President/CEO
WURD Radio LLC

"I am leaving you with a gift-peace of mind and heart.
So don't be troubled or afraid."
—John 14:27 (NLT)

Introduction

This book was written to celebrate and honor super smart, creative kids just like you. I wanted to let you and your parents know that a unique and special destiny is awaiting each one of you. I want you to know beyond the shadow of a doubt that the headlines of today that would lead you to believe that you are somehow a lesser being, somehow the child of a lesser God, is not the truth of who you are. I wrote this book because I want you to know that you are magnificent.

Parts of my own story are interwoven throughout these pages, because I also want you to know that I may be a doctor now, board-certified in family medicine and obesity medicine, but this was not always the case. My first passion and career path was as a dancer and choreographer. When I was 12 years old, I was invited to join my first dance company, The Maureen Deakin Dance Ensemble. Some may find my path to becoming a doctor a bit unusual, however, I have been able to use my journey as a performing artist to become a professional dancer, a choreographer, a doula, and then a doctor.

A lot of the 'how' of that journey has to do with learning to apply the powerful skill of meditation to my life. I want to share that tool and that 'how' with you and your parents in the pages of this book. There are actually several tools that I want to share with you, and I refer to them as Power Keys. Because I want you to become excellent at whatever you choose to do in this world, even at a young age, I will also be assigning homework. This book was conceived over the Martin Luther King weekend in January 2018. In many places people are invited to spend the MLK holiday serving others and participating in a variety of volunteer activities to help others. I often felt that since I had chosen a life of service by going into medicine, that going to work on MLK day was my demonstration of honoring and celebrating the life of this man whose fight for the human rights of African Americans represented a global fight for the rights of all humans.

My hope and expectation at the hospitals and institutions where I worked was that the day would be celebrated and honored, recognized and infused with the spirit of Dr. Martin Luther King. Inspired by his words, "…of all the forms of inequality, injustice in healthcare is the most shocking and inhuman…" MLK, Jr., I decided to begin my career in medicine by caring for and meeting the medical needs of our nation's underserved people. Time and time again, I was underwhelmed. I was disappointed because when I showed up at work on MLK Day, I wanted my workplaces to be having real dialogues and real acknowledgements of the greatness of Martin Luther King, Jr. and the significance of this day in world history. Instead, many of these places thought that having the hospital cafeteria prepare a soul food dinner and posting a few posters with MLK quotes on them would suffice.

I grew weary of overhearing conversations from those who blatantly disrespected Dr. King and went out of their way to belittle the man and his work. I have been in cafeterias on MLK day and overheard resident doctors, who were naturalized American citizens, stating that what MLK did was not that important. I have heard attending physicians chuckle on the way to the operating room and say that if it was up to King and people who think like him, we doctors wouldn't make any money and we would be expected to take care of everyone. (Imagine that, doctors who are expected to take care of people!) I have heard patients say that they hate Dr. King, and wish we could go back to segregated schools and the "good ol' days."

I was also profoundly disappointed that here in America, everything that my parents fought for as far as racial justice, equality, and opportunity seemed to be coming undone. Black people—men and women, boys and girls—were becoming state-sanctioned target practice. I was concerned for my sons who seemed to be growing up in a country that had two destinations in mind for their brilliance: a jail cell or a coffin. This unapologetic hate was not limited to persons living in black and brown bodies, Jewish people were being targeted, those of the Muslim faith were under attack, the LGBTQ community was facing ongoing discrimination and threat, immigrants from many nations were being detained and mistreated, women were under attack, and suicide rates across all groups was rising.

I could hardly recognize this as the America of my hopes and dreams. As fate would have it, a friend and colleague invited me to a weekend retreat called Revisioning Medicine. Interestingly, it took place this year over the MLK weekend in Topanga, CA. I read the description of the retreat, founded and led by author Deena Metzger: Revisioning Medicine is a council that honors and relies on deep dialogue between medical and health practitioners and medicine people—healers, pipe carriers, shamans, energy workers, dreamers, story tellers, sound healers, indigenous elders and practitioners—as peers to address and vision healing with heart, complexity and profundity. Something in my spirit recognized that attending this year's retreat with an international gathering of medical professionals and wisdom traditional healers just might provide me with an opportunity to have in-depth conversations that would have real meaning and feel like an honorable way to spend the Martin Luther King Holiday. I was also hoping for some quiet and solitude so I could hear myself think, remember my dreams and the whispering of my soul, and find a new path forward—away from the disappointments of the election of 2016 and the America I found myself living in.

I was not to be disappointed, as the first words of meditation in a time of madness began to stir in my spirit on that mountain top in California.

That morning in Topanga on that mountaintop, my eyes closed in meditation, I drifted back in time to the evening when I learned that Dr. King had been killed. I was 12 years old, brushing my teeth and listening to my treasured transistor radio when the programming was interrupted to say that Dr. Martin Luther King had died from an assassin's bullet. First I told my mom who was upstairs with me at the time. Her reaction was disbelief.

"Carol, you must have heard wrong."

"No, Mom. I didn't, they are saying it again." I ran downstairs to tell my father, who reacted with stunned silence. My dad, a real foot soldier in the civil rights movement and my hero, simply had no words for the nightmarish news that I was sharing with him. My father, often referred to as a 'race man' by family and close friends, so filled with the powerful rhetoric of freedom and pride that stirred in his soul and that he taught me daily, simply sat in stunned silence with a far-away look in his eyes. Sadly, now I all too often see that same look in the eyes of my son as his contemporaries are gunned down in what seems like a barrage of state-sanctioned murders. I feel that hollow empty look in the pit of my stomach as I fear for the lives of my sons and all of us who inhabit black bodies, brown bodies, Jewish bodies, Muslim bodies, gay bodies, Latinx bodies and all bodies that do not agree with the status quo in what feels like an increasingly hostile territory in my country, the United States of America.

As a 12-year-old girl, I was curious and perplexed, saddened that Mrs. King no longer had a husband and that the King children no longer had a father. I also mourned that I lived in a country that seemed to wish that I didn't really exist. It was my hope that if we kept fighting and kept trying, and if I personally studied hard and excelled, by the time I had my own children, enough like-minded people would have changed the prevailing views on all sides of the equation. I wanted my children to be born in a country that saw and appreciated their value and gave them a chance to excel based on the merit of their character, free from the bondage of institutional and personal racism and hatred.

I grew up with the understanding that I could be murdered, bombed, hosed, spat on, raped, jailed, beaten beyond recognition, and lynched. Yet, I held hope that people like my parents were fighting for me and that one day this would end.

I cannot begin to tell you how disappointed I am, in what I am living in this post-Obama era: "the staggering numbers of black men in jail; the recurrent killings of unarmed black youth by the police; the emboldened presence of white supremacism" (Holland Cotter, *New York Times*, Sunday, April 1, 2018).

Centering myself once more, focused once again on taking quiet, long, even breaths, I continue my reflections on that quiet mountaintop in Topanga, I comfort myself with the words of Dr. King who said, "One day we must come to see that peace is not merely a distant goal that we set but that it is a means by which we arrive at that goal. We must pursue peaceful ends through peaceful means."

In prayer, I hold myself in the perfect peace of love that surpasses all understanding, and I see clearly that the call to action, my charge, is to stand boldly on the promises of the as yet unfinished work of my parents and Dr. King. To call together affinity groups of humans who value diversity, are willing to make change, and, where necessary, reparation to those whose humanity has been historically devalued. To make this nation safe for my children and my children's children. I and all who join with me cannot be defeated. The very soul of humanity is at stake.

Hey kids, parents, guardians, I don't mean to frighten you or upset you in any way. This is my story and perspective. What I would like you to do is to stop reading now and sit together for a few minutes and talk about your family history, your family story. Can you think of a time when either you or someone in your family was treated unkindly or unfairly? Kids, have you ever seen anyone at your school treated unkindly or unfairly because they were somehow different? Parents/Guardians, what about you in your place of work?

How did it make you feel? What did you do about it? How might things have been different? For both kids and parents/guardians: In what ways would you like to change the world?

How to Read this Book

You can read it straight through or you can pick a chapter that looks interesting to you and start there. Each chapter has a central theme or focus and each chapter has some homework or suggestions that you can do on your own as a kid or a parent! The point is to talk, to learn, to grow, and to ask questions…lots of them.

Sacred Rebel: From Dancer to Doula to Doctor

I wanted to include a synopsis of my life story to give my reading audience a peek behind the scenes. Born Carol Andrea Laurette Penn on December 25, 1956, my parents, William Arthur and Alma Laura, a New York City Law Enforcement Officer and a Director of Nursing, wanted a baby girl. As I reflected on the high and low points of my life, I began to realize that I have been quite a rebel, maverick who was often asking the question 'why not' and seeking my own unique pathways in life. I can also see that from an early age, I had an innate ability to look within, to soothe and balance my nervous system, and think creatively. I did not realize it at the time, but I have been practicing meditation most of my life! In my book, *Meditation in a Time of Madness: A Guidebook for Talented Tweens, Teens, their Parents and Guardians Who Need to Thrive*, I have chosen to write about evidence-based practices from globally proven wisdom and healing traditions.

Some of my content topics are

Meditation
Guided imagery
Yoga
QiGong
Prayer
Spiritual Development

These are the tools in my book, referred to as Power Keys, have helped to shape my life through both the highs and the lows.

So what qualifies me to write this book? Besides my professional and educational credentials as a dancer, doctor, educator and international speaker; I have been a kid, adult and a parent. While my story is only one story, perhaps you will find something that relates to the story of your own life and what you are hoping to create or become. I hope you will enjoy and be inspired by some of the high points and low points of my life shared with you on these pages.

Standing on the shoulders of my ancestors, from the shores of Europe and Africa to the harsh fields of enslavement to the liberation born of rebellion from this lineage, I have inherited the light of wisdom, creativity, radical courage, love and respect that have been passed down from the heart of each generation to the next. I align myself with the spirit of sacred rebellion and can look back on my life as a series of synchronous rebellions that have placed me on the path of realizing my God given purpose.

Highlights of my life: Staging my first rebellion at the age of three, at my first dance recital. I had practiced and practiced, I knew my music and my moves forward and backwards. The springtime recital came and it was my turn to perform my first solo. I DID NOT dance! No one had told me that dancing was to be shared in front of anyone. I thought my little tutu and tiara was just for me! (Actually, the teacher had decided to teach me privately because she thought that the parents of the children of European descent would not want their kids in class with me, a little brown girl.)

Another highlight: Seeing my first ballet at age three at the Lincoln Center in NYC, Arthur Mitchell and Suzanne Farrell dancing with New York City ballet and performing works by George Balanchine and the music by Stravinsky! My first dance performance at four after I decided that I would dance in front of other people.

I staged my second rebellion at the age of 5 with my co-conspirator and sister-cousin Beverly, by refusing to participate in a bomb shelter drill at school. My first airplane trip with my grandmother was another highlight and that started a lifelong love affair with travel.

Another highlight: my first film appearance for Scholastic Readers at age 7 and winning my first extemporaneous award for storytelling at the age of 7. Being christened at age 7, so "I would remember" and "like a tree that is planted by the water, (she) shall not be moved." (By then, I was quite renowned for my persistence!) That hymn became my first theme song!

My third rebellion occurred at age 9 when I was sent to the principal's office for lining up the desks in my classroom and pretending that I was a tight rope walker in a circus. My teacher said that my friend Susan and I could not go out for recess because we had been talking in class. When the principal looked in the classroom, there I was walking across the top of the desks.

Sweet childhood memories: My glorious childhood and parents, Alma and Arthur; grandparents, Josephine and George; my half-brother, Arthur; my cousins (more like brothers and sisters); my pets, a beautiful boxer, a delightful calico kitten, and the others that followed; my first garden; and growing up on the banks of a river with the beach and the ocean five minutes away. My father taught me how to ride a horse bareback, box, and shoot a rifle! My junior high and high school performing and athletic career, lettering in track and gymnastics. Being asked to join a dance company at age 12. Winning my first state wide choreographic championship at age 14 with my own choreography.

My next rebellion occurred at my church at age 14: Telling the minister that God speaks to me and through me when I dance, then later being asked to perform my first sacred dance piece and form my first liturgical dance group. Finishing high school in Indonesia and studying Balinese dance in Bali, yoga and meditation.

Staging my next rebellion at age 19: Telling my parents I was going to be a visiting student at NYU for a semester when I was actually transferring to NYU (a more expensive school, besides my parents had sent me to Connecticut College for Women to major in Dance Education and study at the American Dance Festival, held on that campus in the summer months). Many highlights followed: Auditioning for and being accepted on a full scholarship to the Alvin Ailey American Dance Theater school; being an original member of the Alvin Ailey American Dance Theater Workshop Company under the Direction of Kelvin Rotardier; being asked to join the Ailey Children's Faculty by Tom Stevens and Denise Jefferson when I left the workshop company; applying and becoming a Teaching Fellow at the Kennedy Center for the Performing Arts; Founding my company Pennvisions and traveling and touring for the next 10 year with my company, including performing at the White House, teaching throughout the United States and abroad: China, Senegal, Egypt, Scotland, St. Lucia, Hong Kong and Singapore.

There's more: entering a beauty pageant on a whim and winning, becoming Miss Black New York and then becoming first runner up to Miss Black America.

The journey of joy continued with becoming a mom, giving birth to my son, Keita Omowale (KAY-Tah / Oh-moh-walay) meaning: One who has faith, the prince who returns home.

The day I was accepted to medical school, loved medical school, having my son and parents witness my graduation from medical school in 2006. Hated my first year in residency, rebelled here and quit near the end of my first year. Searched for and found my path and direction in medicine with the Center for Mind Body Medicine (www.cmbm.org) and becoming Chief Resident after I returned to finish my graduate medical education.

Co-founding my woman's Dance Company, Core of Fire, after I thought I had retired from dancing, and performing from February 2006-present.

Reconnecting with a dear friend only to discover that he was the one all along, the one my heart was longing for, my soul mate, my one true love, after saying I would never even date again. On August 2, 2014, marrying my best friend and superstar, Mr. Diem Jones. Our boys, Keita and Dima, becoming brothers.

When I reflect back on this path of rebellion and redemption, I realize that in my own way, I have been steadily working my way towards this legacy of light and finally now, feeling comfortable in claiming this legacy.

"We may encounter many defeats but we must not be defeated." —Maya Angelou

Some of the lowest points in my life: The church bombing of the Sunday School in Alabama and the death of the four little girls attending Sunday school in their church basement. One of them was named Carol and we were the same age. From that moment on, I somehow knew that being brown could cost me my life. I soon came to know that it would cost a lot of brown people their lives. My parents were/are activists, and I grew up during the civil rights era.

However, even this frightening awareness that came to me at such a young age has transformed from a low point to a high point, because it is the foundation of awareness that is the cornerstone of my book, *Meditation in a Time Of Madness: A Guidebook for Talented Tweens, Teens, Their Parents and Guardians Who Need to Thrive.* Learning meditation at a young age and really developing the ability to 'be still and know' has allowed me to rise to the occasion and thrive in my own times of illness, heartbreak, disappointments and betrayals, and to stay in touch with my own inner light when all around me was darkness. This has become the skill set that I want to pass on to all children and their parents/guardians.

My purpose in life is simply to know God, to seek, and see the reflection of Universal Love in all.

May you discover yours.

Preface

I am writing this book because I am the mother of two sons. Because on most days I wake up horrified by the news of the day before where someone living in a brown body has been murdered, harmed, jailed, or otherwise made less than human by a society that seems to be hell bent on culturally and institutionally eradicating the humanity of most (if not all) persons of color. I am horrified at what I see and what I hear.

I am writing this book because I do not want to feel helpless in front of some faceless enemy that seems to be both everywhere and nowhere all at once. I am writing this book because I do not want other parents to feel helpless when it seems like there is nothing that can protect our children from this nameless, faceless enemy that has the power to be everywhere yet nowhere simultaneously. I am writing this book because I will not give up my power so easily. I am writing this book because I am not helpless.

I am writing this book because I wanted to share a few tools that helped me when I felt as if I was facing impossible choices, unbearable sorrow, crushing disappointment, divorce, illness, and death. I am writing this book because there are times when we all face the impossible, the improbable, the difficult. And when those times come, we are called upon to be absolutely clear minded, focused and decisiveness. I cannot think of any other time in my life history where the need for a focused and calm mind with the ability to think clearly and act with both decisiveness and compassion is more needed than right now.

It is my desire and prayer to give some parents and their gifted children some tools and guideposts along the way as we learn the power of meditation in a time of madness.

Chapter 1

Communication: Letter to the Kids and Their Parents and Guardians

Dear Kids,

Because you are so super smart and so creative, you are actually gonna teach your parents a lot of what I am talking about in this book.

I look upon each of you as my 'cultural' child. I think kids are super great human beings, and I feel I have learned some of my most powerful life lessons from my students and patients under the age of 10! So thank you for that.

In this book I am hoping to give you some secrets and tools that will help you go far in life, no matter how hard or impossible it might seem at first. One of the first things that I want you to know is that life is not always so much fun and people are not always kind or honest. You are going to run into difficult situations and people, even some big disappointments along the way. At one point you will find out that your parents and grandparents are not perfect people, and while I always hope that they are good to YOU, you may have to learn to forgive mom and dad and other family members as well, even your siblings. Love them anyway, forgive them anyway. Remember, it is as important to learn what not to do as it is to learn what to do. Life and your family and friends will teach you both.

The tools that I am referring to have to do with movement and meditation. We are going to learn that movement is the new medicine, and we'll learn how this new medicine can help us grow in unique and surprising ways. We are also going to learn how meditation helps us heal in mind, body, and spirit to keep moving forward in life. We are going to learn that both movement and meditation are original fundamental medicines that were/are practiced by many indigenous people the world over: Africa, Asia, the Americas, North, South and Central, and Europe. All original people knew that our most powerful medicines were made in our own bodies and minds, and that medicines that we created from plants, herbs, and minerals only worked because they were similarly structured to something we already had inside of our own bodies and minds. Sometimes it seems that we have forgotten certain fundamental truths about medicine and our bodies, so I hope this book will help you remember and live these truths.

I do believe in a Higher Power. I believe in God and just as God loves us, God wants us to love ourselves. So, in that way, you are never alone. This Higher Power has given us a few gifts to make sure we can understand that we are never alone. In this book, I hope to share those gifts and guidance with you and your parents.

Dear Parents/Guardians,

So you have been blessed to have stewardship over your super smart creative kid(s). Congratulations! Kids really are the greatest of gifts and blessings!

My hope in writing this book and sharing some of my insights and stories is that you will be inspired to work with your children and share these secrets of life. My wish is that you will also find the ideas in these pages inspiring and encouraging for you to have a more fulfilled life and to truly walk in your own purpose.

The first thing I want you to do is to read the letter that I wrote your kids, and I want you to remember something that my father often would say to me: Kids don't really remember what you tell them to do, but they do remember what you show them how to do and if you show them how to be. Thanks, dad. As always, your words are with me on a daily basis.

Parents/guardians, you may be thinking, "What does this woman know? She's a doctor. She has published a book! What could she possibly know of hard, challenging or disappointing times?" Please read my story that I have shared at the beginning of this book. I, just like you, have gone through my dark days, my days of despair and profound disappointment; that's called life. However, I do credit the tools I have shared in this book as my blueprint for success no matter how the external circumstances have presented themselves. And guess what? It is the very nature of life itself to cycle through difficult times, disappointing times, hard times. Hopefully after reading this book, you will free yourself from being trapped in the cycle of disappointment by applying some of the techniques and suggestions that I make in this book.

Enjoy exploring these pages together with your super smart creative kid(s). Remember your kids will walk in their purpose when you walk in yours. Teach, don't preach, and be the change you want to see in the world.

Good clear open loving communication can be a lifelong gift between parent and child. It a Power Key that can be cultivated at home on a daily basis. When the family has a meal together, make it a habit to put away all electronic devices and spend the meal time talking to each other. Begin the meal by expressing gratitude.

Homework Kids: Write a letter to your parents, letting them know what you are grateful for and why. Read your letter aloud to your parent/guardian.

Homework Parents: Write a letter to your kids, letting them know what you are grateful for and why. Read your letter aloud to your kid(s).

Chapter 2

Love: Be Still and Know

Kids: Do you know how loved you are? How valuable and irreplaceable you are? I mean, do you really know? A big part of my prayer is that, if you do not know it now, you will know it by the time you finish reading this book and following some of the suggestions and guidelines contained in these pages. You are so awesome, so magnificent, cherished beyond your wildest imagination. You are supposed to feel these things each and every day. In case you don't, let me start pointing out some small things to you.

You know that breath you just took? Breathe in, breathe out. Yup, that's love! Put your hand on your heart. Feel that, *lub dub, lub dub*—your heart beat—yup, that's love! You know that dream you had last night? The one when you woke up smiling? Yup, that's love! And oh yeah, that hug that mom or dad gave you? That's love too. The nice lady that smiles at you every time you go in her store? Yeah, that's love too.

Love is really all around you all the time. In some situations, it does not always come from the direction or person that convention tells us it should be coming from, and that's unfortunate because that can be a trap. The flowers are blooming, and we see their bright brilliant color. That's love. Instead of seeing that, we focus on the boy or the girl that won't return our affection. We have a warm sweater and eat our favorite meal, yet we can't feel that love because we are fixated on not making the track team, or, for working folks, not getting the promotion. With all of this focus outside of ourselves, no wonder we miss the mark, we miss the love. A great reason to learn how to meditate is that we learn to recognize and see the love when and where it is coming and let go of our attachment to where the love is not coming from.

It took me quite a while to learn this lesson and I am still working on the subtleties of it, but man oh man, when the love is not there, I have learned to let go of my attachments and move on fast to keep walking in my purpose. As Desmond Tutu and the 14th Dalai Lama have written in *The Book of Joy*:

"Discovering more joy does not save us from the inevitability of hardship and heartbreak. In fact, we may cry more easily, but we will laugh more easily too. Perhaps we are just more alive. As we discover more joy, we can face suffering in a way that enables rather than embitters. We have hardships without becoming hard. We have heartbreaks without being broken."

Yup, all that is love too.

Learn to be still and know this truth.

Homework Kids:
Write down 5 things that make you feel happiest, safest, loved. Share your list and discuss with your parent/guardian.

Homework Parents:
Write down 5 things that make you feel happiest, safest, loved. Share your list and discuss with your kid(s).

Chapter 3

Purposeful Meditation

This is it. This is where you find the calm in the eye of the storm. For kids, is the storm bullying at school? Is the storm failing grades or tough classes? Is the storm feelings of depression or sadness? For adults, is the storm a failing relationship, work-related stress, care-taker stress, or even a general dissatisfaction with life, your own sadness and depression?

THREE MAJOR FORMS OF MEDITATION

So often I hear, "I just can't seem to meditate." Many people have a fixed idea in their head that tells them that successful meditation looks like a person sitting perfectly still, on a mountain top with their legs crossed or folded under them. Too bad, because that's not necessarily meditation either. Meditation means to be in a state of relaxed awareness, and there are many ways to achieve a state of relaxed awareness!

This state of relaxed awareness has a special place in our brain. It's called our autonomic nervous system, and it has two parts: 1) a sympathetic part, we know as flight, fight, or freeze and 2) a parasympathetic part, we know as rest and relax. The job of meditation is to bring these two parts into balance. When we need to heal, meditation helps to bring the parasympathetic aspect to the forefront, so good thoughts, calmness, and our body's own healing chemistry can take over. Sometimes the hardest part of learning how to meditate is discovering which form of meditation is the best one for us. Did you know that there are three major approaches to meditation? Let's discover one you might like.

EXPRESSIVE MEDITATION

This is perhaps the oldest form of meditation, and it involves movement. Have you ever put on your favorite dance music and just danced and sang until you were out of breath (probably with a great big smile on your face with the music turned way up loud)? How did you feel afterwards? If you are like me, you most likely felt great! The smile on your face probably stayed there for a while, and whatever you had to do next went off without a hitch.

Well that's a form of meditation, and the resulting feeling of flow or being in flow that comes out of it is the benefit of it. Some other forms of expressive meditation you have also heard of, and maybe even already have tried, consist of yoga, Tai chi/qigong or even Pilates. Notice how in these forms of movement, the movement and the breath are closely linked, and often it is the use of the breath that initiates or starts the movement. More about the use of the breath in the following chapter.

CONCENTRATIVE MEDITATION

Another major form of meditation is something called Concentrative meditation. Ever said a prayer and then repeated it several times and felt a sense of calm or peace come over you afterwards? Ever repeated the Lord's Prayer or said the Rosary over and over again? Yup, all forms of Concentrative meditation, which is usually a repeated phrase said over and over again for three minutes, five minutes, 10 minutes, 20 minutes, or longer. Try saying something to yourself like: Breathe in calm, breathe out anger, breathe in love, breathe out hate, breathe in energy, breathe out tired (and then repeat). Do this until you feel good and for as long as it feels good. You can even set a timer or an alarm on your phone for 5 or 10 minutes, just to try it out.

MINDFUL MEDITATION

Another type of meditation is called Mindful Meditation. A lot of people really like this one. Here we learn how to concentrate or focus on what we are doing in the moment, how to really pay attention on purpose and even come to enjoy it. So, for example, when eating a meal, try just eating your meal with no distractions like texting, watching a show, doing your homework, or talking on the phone. Just eat. This is called Mindful Eating. Try eating a meal this way and notice how the food tastes!

Homework Kids:

This week, do a little research and try each different type of meditation approaches. If you have never been in a yoga class, try that. For concentrative meditation, try one of the phrases that I suggested; set a timer and see how you feel. When thoughts come, let them come, and go right back to repeating your phrase. Finally, try to eat a meal with no distractions and then pay attention to how you feel afterwards.

Homework Parents:

Your homework is the same as the kids. In addition to doing all of the above, I would like you to create an opportunity for your family to eat a mindful meal together. It doesn't have to be the entire meal. Try spending at least a part of the meal in silence after saying a grace or blessing over the food. If keeping a few moments of silence while everyone is eating is too difficult at first, ask everyone to share something that they are grateful for, even if just for that day. And make sure there are no electronics—phones, iPads, etc.—anywhere in sight!

Chapter 4

The Breath

LEARNING TO BREATHE: BASIC PHYSIOLOGY OF BREATH

Your breath is your best friend and guide on this journey to the inner self. Now most of us take our breath for granted until something happens and we have less of it. Then we really notice! One of the sites that has always moved me to tears is a baby taking its first breath. I find this a deeply spiritual moment.

At one time, my career aspiration was to become an obstetrician/gynecologist. I did several sub-internships in this medical specialty, and before entering medical school, I worked as a childbirth educator and a doula, so I have been privileged to attend quite a few births. As the baby emerges from the womb, there is often a hush that falls over the room. Even if it's the briefest of moments, I would notice it every time. All eyes are on the baby, often still, colorless and sometimes a bit blue. The baby's tiny body immediately responds to the atmospheric pressure and the forces of gravity, eyes flutter open, arms stretch wide, nostrils flare, color begins to come to the skin, a slight gasp, a startled look, followed by the infant's cry of life! When I would glance about the room, tears would often be in everyone's ones, with the newly born's parents having tears of joy and relief streaming down their faces. Never a jaded moment.

It is one of the moments for me when I have felt most alive in the world, when I have felt the presence of God walking all over me and all around the room. Here's an interesting fact: Whenever one women is giving birth, approximately 350,000 women around the world are simultaneously giving birth. You see, we are truly never alone. We have God moments like this available to us at any given moment. For just a moment, close your eyes and see if you can imagine yourself as a newborn baby taking your first breath.

SOFT BELLY BREATHING

Breathing is our Power Key #4! Our breath, governed by our autonomic nervous system, is something that we have a small amount of partial control over. Have you ever tried holding your breath until you pass out? You can't do it, right? That's because our breath is fundamental to our very survival: all of our bodily functions, all of our cellular functions, our brain functions, even our molecular and genetic functions because of it. In other words nothing, and I mean absolutely nothing, happens without respiration or more simply put…breath.

So while we cannot control our breath, we can learn to regulate it and use it in a way to enhance our ability to function on many levels. One way is to learn a great technique called 'soft belly' breathing. Soft belly breathing is actually a form of concentrative meditation where, after we settle down a bit, we repeat to ourselves the phrase "soft belly" over and over again. Soft belly breathing is one of my favorite ways to meditate because it taps directly into the brain and the vagus nerve helping us to communicate along something called the gut brain axis.

Our vagus nerve (sounds like vagabond or the wanderer) actually innervates or carries signals to very important organs in our body like the carotid body in the neck, the heart, lungs, stomach, large and small intestines, etc. Whatever information the vagus nerve picks up in its journey from the brain to take to these organs and structures, it is also picking up information to carry back to the brain. All this activity affects the choices we make, how we feel, and even whether or not we are making fat or building muscle mass! So you can see why it is important to have our autonomic nervous system well-tuned and in balance. Soft belly breathing can help us do that. Let's learn how.

Start by getting comfortable. So for now let's say that you are going to sit in your favorite chair.

Close your eyes and notice your breath, the air going in and going out of your nostrils. Get curious about the miracle of your own breath!

Let the muscles around your forehead and eyes relax. Let the muscles around your jaw, cheeks, and chin relax. Even let your tongue relax; it's a muscle too.

Place one hand on your stomach and feel the rise and fall of your breath with each inhalation and each exhalation. As you inhale, repeat the word 'soft.' As you exhale, say the word 'belly.' Repeat this phrase silently to yourself with each breathing cycle, doing so at your own rate, rhythm and timing.

Now if some other thoughts pop into your mind, that's okay. Let them come because it is the nature of the mind after all to think; just go back to paying attention to your breath or repeating the phrase 'soft belly.' If this is your first time trying this type of breathing, maybe try for 3-5 minutes. How do you feel? Is it hard, is it easy? Try it by yourself and try it with maybe your mom or dad.

THREE-PART BREATHING

If you found 'soft belly' breathing a little difficult, or maybe even silly or funny, here's another approach to getting familiar and comfortable with your breath that falls under the category of mindful meditation. Here we will learn how to utilize all the zones of our lungs, creating greater mental clarity and even improving our digestive processes.

You can do this sitting, standing or lying down. Let's try this one lying down, but don't fall asleep! We are going to use a position called the constructive rest position. Lie down on your back and bend your knees, placing your feet on the floor. Now instead of placing one hand on your belly as you did in soft belly breathing, place both hands on your belly. Breathe in, breathe out and notice how your belly rises right into your hands. Breathe and relax for a few breaths and notice how you feel. Try to breathe so deeply that you notice how even your back muscles seem to move and relax with each breath.

Next, move your hands up to your rib cage. Again, breathe in, breathe out, and notice that when you breathe deeply your ribs expand sideways. Continue to let your belly rise and fall even with your ribs moving now. Relax between each breath and notice how you feel.

Now move your hands all the way up to your collar bones and breathe so deeply that you feel your upper chest move right into your hands. Take a few more breaths just like this. Notice how your entire chest and belly is rising and falling with each breath. You are using your entire lung capacity to breathe, maximizing the circulation of oxygen and nutrients throughout your entire body! Many of us have gotten into poor breathing habits or patterns of only using a part of our lung capacity to breathe. When we learn how to use more of our lung capacity to breathe, we help to reduce pain in our body, improve sleep, increase our ability to focus, and increase our energy.

CHAOTIC BREATHING

This breath, called chaotic breathing, is a form of expressive meditation. Basically what I want you to try in this breath is to pretend you are a chicken. Bend your elbows and tuck your right hand under your right axilla (arm pit) and do the same on your left side. Now flap your wings and blow out of your nose as hard as you can every time you flap your wings. You will really be getting out a lot of stale air and waste product when you breathe in this manner. I love to put on some drumming music and do this one to the music. When you first start, try to do this for five minutes, but stop if you feel dizzy or faint. You can also always slow down and take a break and then continue after taking a few normal breaths. Some ancient people used to call chaotic breathing "skull shining breath," because it can make you sweat on top of your head! Notice what you feel when you stop—energy, a certain sense of peace, calm, some even say strength.

ALTERNATE NOSTRIL BREATHING

Alternate nostril breathing is an intermediate or advanced breathing practice that is really excellent for bringing balance and healing to the whole system. Alternate nostril breathing is one of my favorite Power Keys for whenever I have to study for a very hard test. Here's how to do it: If you are right handed, try doing the breathing first with the right hand. If left handed, try your left hand first. I will teach you the technique using your right hand. You guessed it, I am right handed. Sorry to you lefties out there! Either hand can work though.

Let's try: Take your right hand and put your second and third fingers on the bridge of your nose; now take your ring finger and little finger and close off your left nostril. Breathe in through your right nostril. Take your thumb and close off your right nostril, release your ring finger and little finger, and exhale out of the left nostril. Now breathe in through your left nostril, close it off and lift your thumb, and exhale out of the right nostril. That's it. I think you have it. Do this for a few rounds or cycles. Sit quietly and then return to your normal way of breathing. Whenever I have to concentrate or think more clearly, I will do this for 5 or even 10 minutes.

Homework Kids:

For now, we are complete with our discussion on breathing. Learning and practicing these few techniques will help you over and over again. Try doing all of these breathing techniques at least three times. For now, pick the one you like best and then practice that technique for one week. Discuss with your parent(s)/guardian what breathing technique they like the best and why. Try teaching each other the techniques.

Homework Parents:
Be sure to try these techniques on yourself. Breaths like soft belly and three-part breathing, because they are so efficient in balancing the autonomic nervous system and can even help you to lose those stubborn pounds you have been holding onto, especially the stress-induced belly fat.

Meditation is a very powerful tool meant to be used everyday and in many different situations. The next time you feel afraid or nervous or you hear something scary on the news, try the soft belly breathing that you learned earlier in the chapter. Here's an easy version: sit comfortably and when you are ready, gently close your eyes. Begin to notice or concentrate on your breath; breathe in, breathe out. If thoughts come, let them come, but see if you can watch your thoughts drift by like clouds drifting by in the sky. Go back to your breath and see if you can notice the air coming into your nostrils. The next time you breathe in, say to yourself the word soft and when you breathe out say the word belly. Quietly repeat the phrase 'soft belly' silently to yourself with every in and out breath: "Soft belly, soft belly" at your own rate, rhythm, and timing. Do this alone, together as a family, or anytime you want to feel calm and safe.

Chapter 5

Ascending to the Throne of Your Well-Being

GROUNDING

Once we have learned how to tune into our breath, the next step is to learn how to ground or anchor ourselves. One of my favorite ways to ground myself is quite literally to stomp my feet, purposefully, to notice and connect a physical part of myself with the earth. There is also the mental, psychological, and spiritual aspect of grounding yourself. Remember, our fundamental definition of meditation is to be in a state of relaxed awareness, so it is very important to give ourselves the gift of meditation each and every day. In theory, one can be in a meditative state at all times. It is from this place of relaxed awareness that we make our best decisions. We gain mental clarity, our bodies are able to heal, and we are able to recognize and tap into our own super powers, develop them, and enhance them. Hence, learning to take our seat is our Power Key 5.

TAKING YOUR SEAT ON YOUR THRONE

Many people hold a picture in their mind of meditating while being in a seated position. However, while one can meditate in a variety of positions, achieving this state of relaxed awareness can be enhanced if we take our time coming into a seated position. Seated meditation is often how I start out or open up my yoga classes. I invite everyone to imagine that they are royalty. How would you sit if you were a king or a queen? Would people know that you were a special person just by looking at you? Would you look elegant, regal, serene, intelligent? Hmmm… I wonder. Our seated posture in meditation helps our body and brain to optimize its own physiology.

Let's try: I invite you to place the soles of your feet on the floor, remember our grounding practice of stomping our feet? Our legs are not crossed, our ankles are not crossed. If we were outdoors, I would say really sink your feet down onto the ground and feel the grass or the sand between your toes. Become aware that your own energy field or electromagnetic forces extend at least three feet beneath your feet. Soon you will become aware that there is a slight tension or charge in your legs as you press your feet against a firm surface.

Allow your weight to be evenly distributed over your sitting bones. Lengthen your spine from the base of your tailbone up through your lower back, mid back, upper back and finally your neck. Feel the energy going through the crown of your head. Your spine is now elongated and quite elegant. With this long fluid spine, your lungs can completely relax and expand in the cavity of your torso because you have made more room for them. Your hands are placed comfortably in your lap, palms may be turned down or turned up. Palms turned up signify an attitude of receptivity, so you might want to experiment with what that feels like and what that brings to your spirit.

Take a moment to notice how your body feels right now. Notice your breath. Breathe in and out through your nose. Notice your breath. Stay in tune with your breath. I mean, really get fascinated with your breath. Breathing in, breathing out, breathing in, breathing out. Your quiet measured breaths are your friend and guide to creating this state of relaxed awareness. Do you know that there are even some wisdom teachings that suggest that in between the in breath and the out breath, there is a pause, and it is there at that pause where we meet God?

Breathing in, breathing out, breathing in and breathing out. Now become aware of the energy coming up from the crown of your head. Understand that your personal electromagnetic field extends not only three feet below your feet but likewise at least three feet above your head. This electromagnetic field also extends three feet in front of you and behind you as well. Think of your electromagnetic field as a sea of molecules that is all around you. It is like an ocean that we are floating in every day. Take a moment now to imagine that above you and below, and 360 degrees around you, you are completely and totally supported. You are sitting in and folded in an envelope of love, deeply loving support. Imagine that there are young kings and queens just like you all over the world connecting heart to heart, connecting to your heart. All of these connected hearts create a unified force field. You are sitting on the edge of evolutionary consciousness and connecting loving energy, resources and light. We breathe in and we breathe out, staying present to the breath. Feel a sense of inner space and become aware of all that is above, below, in front of you, in back of you and to the right and to the left of you.

THREE-MINUTE MEDITATION

Young king or queen, emperor or empress, seated properly on your throne, seated fully in your power, continue your focus on your breath for three full minutes. If your mind starts to wander and your thoughts insist on bubbling up, that's okay! Watch your thoughts like a cloud drifting by in a bright blue sky and then go right back to your breathing. Also, if your mind wanders (and it will), or thoughts come (and they will), try this mindful approach and go through the step by step process of how to sit upon your throne.

LASER FOCUS

One of the greatest results of this type of meditation will be your ability to have a laser sharp focus. The kind of focus that is required in school to absorb lessons in math and the sciences as well as to remember and to interpret what you read. Experiment with doing the meditation with varying lengths of time and see for yourself.

GETTING PAST OUR INNER GATE KEEPER

One of the other great benefits of doing this type of meditation is when we need to do some creative problem solving or when we need some encouragement. Have you ever noticed that sometimes when you come up with a great idea, a few minutes later you end up talking yourself out of it? Or you keep struggling to come up with any idea at all? The reason for this is that our brain has a protective built-in mechanism called an ego. It is the job of our ego to maintain the status quo of ourselves. Our ego simply wants to protect what is. After all, what already is works, and, in that moment, you are alive and all systems are functioning. The ego, while necessary, does not like change. Well that's great if you never want to change, grow or try new things. I like to call the ego, our Inner Gate Keeper. Practicing this meditation helps us to get behind and beyond our Inner Gate Keeper.

Homework Kids and Parents:

Practice this approach to meditation first thing in the morning for five minutes each time. Go ahead and take a seat on your throne and watch what happens during the rest of your day. In the evening or before bed, write down three things you want to accomplish on the next day. Repeat every morning for a least one week and keep noticing what happens each day.

I really like to approach my evening meditation using the image of taking a seat on my throne. Kids, sometimes after a hard day at school or if someone bullies you or you feel disappointed in any way, it is wonderful to imagine yourself as a king or a queen—strong, proud, loving, and kind toward yourself and others. Notice how much strength you have in your body, notice how you feel better the more you lengthen your spine. Taking the seat on your throne can help you to remember the truth of who you are: magnificent, brave, unique. As for parents and guardians, # ditto, repeat.

Chapter 6

Sweet Sleep

CREATING YOUR SLEEP ENVIRONMENT

Sleep is a major Power Key! Without the proper amount of rest and sleep, the body and brain simply don't work as well as they could. To maximize all of your super powers, you need to learn how to master the fine art of sleeping and sleeping well.

Here's a guide to how much sleep you generally should be getting:

- Older adults (65 and over): 5-9 hours
- Most adults 26-64 years old: 6-10 hours
- Young adults 18-25 years old: 6-11 hours
- Teenagers 14-17 years old: 7-11 hours
- School age 6-13 years of old: 7-12 hours
- Preschool 3-5 years old: 8-14 hours
- Toddlers 1-2 years old: 9-16 hours
- Infants 4-11 months: 10-18 hours
- Newborns age 0-3 months: 11-19 hours

The recommended ranges for each group are somewhere in the middle, so think of taking off the low number and the high number. Most of us will fall right in the middle somewhere. The message is that human beings need sleep, and every individual has an appropriate number of hours that allows their body and brain to recharge and refuel.

SLEEP HYGIENE

Sleep hygiene refers to creating an environment that is conducive to sleep. There are a couple of pointers here that will help to make you successful in your quest for mastering the Power Key of sleep. Kids, parents and guardians follow the following six steps to your sweeties dreams:

1. No electronics in the bedroom; the bedroom is for sleeping! That means no TV, No iPad, no computer, no phone! If you need an alarm clock, something that wakes you up to sounds of nature or to different shades of light is okay. Anything else actually interferes with the activity of the brain and can reduce optimal function.

2. Turn off electronics at least an hour before your bedtime. If you need to read, read from a book, not an electronic device.

3. Establish a bedtime ritual, one that allows your brain and body to begin to relax and calm down. Try taking a warm shower or even better soaking in a warm tub of water for about 20 minutes. To add some extra relaxation, try putting a cup of baking soda in the water along with a cup of Epsom salts. If you like a cup of warm herbal tea,

something like Egyptian chamomile can be a delightful way to wind down even more.

4. Wear pajamas! I am a big fan of pajama wear. Putting on actual pajamas after bathing in the evening can also be a big signal to your brain and body that it is that special time of night called bedtime.

5. Make sure your bedroom is dark and cool, which is another signal to the brain and body that it is time to sleep.

6. Your bed needs to have a firm mattress and pillow that allows your body to really let go and rest and be supported.

SLEEP WEAR

For real super power sleep, we want super power pajamas. Since sleep is so central to both maximizing our learning capabilities and healing, our sleep wear should support these functions. Ideally, sleep wear should be 100% organic cotton with no artificial dyes or colors. And if you wear underwear or socks to sleep in, they should also be 100% cotton with no artificial dyes or colors.

THE BEST BED

Our beds and bedding should also be of the highest quality. We spend approximately 1/3 of our lives sleeping. Anything we spend that much time doing is worth investing in for our own self-care. Kids, you may not be working now, but you can certainly help your parents learn about sleep, sleep wear, beds and bedding. Our bedding, pillows, sheets, blankets and comforters should be of the best quality possible. Again, organic cotton bedding with pillows that are stuffed with a hypoallergenic material are optimal. Our sheets and pillow cases should be washed on a weekly basis. Kids, you can certainly help do the laundry. Try to use an unscented non-toxic detergent to wash your bedding.

Remember the story of Goldilocks and the Three Bears? Well when it comes to picking out the ideal bed, we have to be just like Goldilocks and literally try the bed and mattress for comfort and support. I know I prefer a mattress that is not too soft, nor one that is super firm. Something in the middle is usually just right for me and guarantees me the best chance of a great night's sleep.

YOGA NIDRA

Yoga nidra means yoga sleep, and it combines mindful meditation using a type of guided imagery and a form of concentrative meditation and/or something called autogenics. Done for about 20 minutes, it is said that a yoga nidra done well is the equivalent of sleeping for three hours. Mastering yoga nidra was one of my secrets for getting through my residency training that so often required staying up most, if not all, of the night for several nights in a row. Learning yoga nidra gives a whole new meaning to the word power nap!

Here's a simple yoga nidra that you can try either by yourself or with a parent or guardian with one person reading the phrases and the other person relaxing. Now the phrases that I am going to ask you to learn and repeat are autogenic phrases. That means that you will be giving suggestions to your self (auto) to aid in your deep relaxation (genic[s]). So you're teaching yourself or making suggestions back to your self in a way to improve your health and ability to rest.

First lie in a comfortable position. Now here are six phrases I would like you to learn to aid in your beginner's yoga nidra:

1. My feet and legs are heavy and warm. I feel completely relaxed.
2. My hands and arms are heavy and warm. I feel completely relaxed.
3. My belly is soft and warm. I feel completely relaxed.
4. My back is long and supple. I feel completely at ease.
5. My lips are soft and full. I feel completely at ease.
6. My forehead is cool. I am at peace.

Repeat each phrase quietly to yourself six times each before moving on to the next one. Try recording yourself in your smart phone so you don't have to be concerned with memorizing the phrases.

DREAM JOURNAL

Another wonderful gift to give yourself is learning how to keep a dream journal. We all dream every night. However, we all don't always remember our dreams. Keeping a dream journal is one way to learn how to remember our dreams and (more importantly) learn from them. Another important aspect of dreams is that they occur beyond the reach of the

Inner Gate Keeper. There are two aspects of dreams that are very empowering. There are personal dreams that are meant just for us, to teach us something, to solve a problem, to help bring something into being. Then there are dreams that come to us and through us that are meant to solve problems or to bring messages into the greater world. I have come to think of this as dreaming on behalf of the collective. I think this is really cool because that means any one of us can solve some of the world's biggest problems and help all of humanity!

Homework Kids and Parents:
Do you realize you can make up your own autogenic phrases? Try making up your own phrases and you may find them even more effective for you. Kids, parents and guardians, try making up some phrases together. Keep them short and simple, and remember you are designing them to help ease you into deep relaxation.
Also, get a journal and put the journal on the table or nightstand by your bed. Leave a couple of pens there as well. When you wake up, just start writing and let your hand move across the paper. Don't think. Just write and see what your dream wants to reveal to you. Try this every morning for the next seven mornings.

Chapter 7

Proper Nutrition: We Really Are What We Eat

Let food by thy medicine. Food and water are absolutely essential for great mental and physical health. The sooner you learn this, the sooner you can learn about what foods are healthiest and the better, stronger, and smarter you will be. Each Power Key fits like a lock in a key with the other Power Keys. In this chapter, we will be exploring how to best get started on optimizing your eating behaviors for maximum health and well-being.

DRAW YOUR RELATIONSHIP WITH FOOD

Try this little exercise. Gather the following materials:

- one or two sheets of 8.5 x 11 white or off-white paper
- some colored pens and crayons and/or markers
- a timer

Set the timer for 15- 20 minutes and draw your relationship with food. There is no right or wrong way to do this. Just let your hand move across the paper and draw how you feel about food, or maybe you will use your imagination and draw how food feels about you!

MINDFUL EATING

"Mindful eating is the practice of cultivating an open-minded awareness of how the food we choose to eat affects one's body, feelings, mind, and all that is around us." [Definition of Mindful Eating/Lexicon of Food]

Mindful eating is a type of meditation. Remember that a meditative state of being can be anything that puts you into a state of relaxed awareness. Being in a state of relaxed awareness is the best way to digest our food! Think about all the things that cause us to have a stomach ache or an upset stomach: eating too much, eating when we don't feel well, or eating when we are angry, tired, sad.

Read my personal account with my first experience with mindful eating. The newfound awareness opened my eyes to all the ways I could change my relationship to food and how this could impact my health and well-being. The participants were asked to select one item then wait for further instructions once everyone had made their choice. What follows describes a personal journey that has forever changed my relationship with food.

Holding the small piece of food first in one hand and then the other, I notice how little it weighs, hardly anything at all. I change it to one hand and then the other, noticing how easy it is to encompass the entire piece with just two fingers. Its oval shape is smooth, except for what feels like a ragged edge on one end; this must have been where she was attached to the vine. I am not sure why, but I have the distinct feeling that my food is female. Perhaps many of the hands that touched her to bring her from the West coast to the East coast were female, or maybe it's simply residual feminine energy from the last pair of hands to touch her. I don't know, but this food in that place in my body where I 'feel' things is decidedly feminine. Holding her up to the light, I notice that she is a beautiful spring-like green, almost translucent, and I can see in her skin a slight veining that's a slightly lighter shade of green. Gently placing the item of food against my lips, right in the center, touching both the upper and lower lip simultaneously, a surprising jolt of feeling startles me as the lightness of the pressure tickles. I feel the sensation in my neck across my back and into my shoulders. It tickles, surprises, startles me, and my eyes fly open. Into my mouth goes the food. At first, there is no taste, her skin protecting her. However, I notice she feels round in my mouth, smooth, some texture, some resistance but not much as my front teeth easily break the skin and her sweetness and moisture cause a burst of wetness to spring forth from my own salivary glands. Instructed to chew longer than usual, soon my entire mouth is alive with a refreshing sweetness that tastes like a spring morning at sunrise. My mouth is cool. The food keeps getting softer and smaller, and each morsel tastes sweeter than the next. Finally, I am allowed to swallow and I notice that I can still taste that amazing sensation of sweetness all the way on the back of my tongue, even at the top of my esophagus as I swallow. She is making her way to my stomach and so are all the hands that prepared her for her journey to nourish my body. She is going and so is all of her history and the history of the vine she grew on, the history of the soil she was planted in, the history of the hopes and the dreams of the people who tilled the soils of her orchard. Sitting quietly now, most sensation gone, I notice that I am in deep heart-centered gratitude for my relationships to people, to the earth and nature, all from one grape.

Kids and adults, try eating one or two meals a week or even one small food item like a grape or a peace of chocolate, mindfully. Kind of like I did in my story. If you are struggling with a few extra pounds, we know that eating mindfully, we eat about 20 % less than we normally would eat. And people actually begin to shed some extra pounds.

GRATITUDE

The practice of gratitude helps us in so many ways. What are you grateful for right now? Do you know that feeling of gratitude actually helps our bodies and brains release healing peptides and neurotransmitters that help us to be well in mind, body, and spirit? Everyday and every night we have opportunities to be thankful. A great way to practice gratitude is at every mealtime; offer a prayer of thanksgiving over your food and anything else you want to be thankful for in that moment. A very good friend of mine keeps a large gratitude vase or jar on her dining room table. There are scraps of paper of varying sizes on a nearby side table along with some pens. Everyday at a set time, she, her three kids and her husband, write down their 'gratefuls' and drop their grateful message into the vase. Whenever the family gathers for meals, someone will reach into the vase and randomly select a 'grateful' that they then read out loud as the blessing for that particular meal. It is a beautiful rich tradition. What gratitude ritual can you think of to do with your family?

FOOD PREP FOR THE WEEK

Think about the following things next time you are in a grocery store or a restaurant. In creating a new relationship with food, it is important to not only rely on common sense but to remember a few basic principles of good nutrition such as the following:

- Eat real food: food that has to be refrigerated and that you have to prepare.
- Eat more whole plant foods: fresh fruit and vegetables, whole grains like brown rice, nuts and seeds.
- Eat more fish and chicken and less red meat.
- Eat a rainbow diet: a wide variety of fruits and vegetables of different colors.
- Avoid processed foods, which contain unhealthy additives.
- Notice when you are full.
- Be aware of how food makes you feel physically and emotionally.

What follows are two learning stories. The first story shows how food is very much a part of both culture and identity, and it also draws from my experience as a doctor who specializes in non-surgical bariatric medicine or obesity medicine. The second story highlights how emotions and traumas can lead to eating choices that can be a part of illness.

Rice And Gravy, Love and Spirit; A Mind Body Medicine Group for Persons Living With Morbid Obesity

Today was the first of eight sessions in a Philadelphia-based private medical practice where I am implementing an evidence-based treatment protocol, utilizing the framework of the shared medical appointment and the center's small group model. The common diagnosis for this group was Morbid Obesity with a BMI of >40. Four participants began today, and the BMI range was from 42-54. The age range was from 30-57. Other co-morbidities included diabetes type 11, chronic kidney disease, osteoarthritis, hypertensive heart disease, chronic bronchitis, chronic pain syndrome and peripheral vascular disease. All of these group participants have tried multiple diets. Two of the five (including myself) had experienced success with weight loss, but always put the weight back on, and then would gain even more weight. One had never tried to lose weight and another had tried multiple times but never lost any weight.

For the check-in, I asked each person to share why they had come to the group and what they would like to take away from their participation. The group was composed of three women and one man. Each took turns introducing themselves and their goals. Shy at first, but as we went around, common themes began to surface, smiles, and then laughter swelled in the group. As each member disclosed their struggles with food, a common theme emerged about the joy and comfort of food, love of sweets, and common ethnic roots with four of the five of us hailing from the Gullah Geechee culture where food is not considered a meal unless rice is served with gravy. More than the rice and gravy, this food ties us to our cultural heritage, crossing oceans and tying us to our African ancestry. Lives and memories are built around the perfect preparation and presentation of rice with well-seasoned gravy, served with a generous portion of cornbread on the side. It is more than mere comfort food; it is a sacrament that ties us to our family roots and symbolizes family bonding, family connection, and ancient tribal memories. These tribal memories have recessed to a place beyond words, but the food calls forth something intangible and unspoken, yet palpable in our hearts and souls. So how does one cut off a lifeline, even when one has identified that on certain levels it is no longer good for you?

One member shared that she recently was able to lose 11 pounds when she stopped eating all refined carbohydrates and only allowed herself to eat her favorites—rice and gravy, pasta, and bread—on Sundays. She shared that during the soft belly breathing, she was softly praying and asking God to help her get control over her desire to constantly eat large portions. She has seen female relative after female relative develop diabetes, felt this was her date with destiny, and wanted to break the cycle.

Another group member shared that she had seen an aunt reverse her diabetes, and she wanted to do the same, although with a BMI of 54 and a recent 30-pound weight gain, she knew she needed to do something more than 'try' to lose weight one more time. She said her reason for being in the group was simple: She was not ready to die at 57. "This is a start in my working on me. It's good to see that other people have the same kind of struggles that I have and to know that you can't give up, and just coming here gives me hope I will reach my goal in getting control over my life. This body is my temple and I want a renewed spirit living in a healthier temple."

And so, another Mind Body Medicine journey has begun for this group and lives are ready to be transformed and temples rebuilt.

The Convergence of Depression, Trauma, and Obesity

Long before I was a board-certified family medicine physician involved with obesity medicine, I was a teaching fellow and performing arts consultant, working for the Kennedy Center for the Performing Arts in their Very Special Arts Program. I was charged on this occasion to travel to a remote and rural area of Vermont to do a week-long workshop for a local school district, working with classroom teachers, physical education teachers, and administrators on how to integrate dance into the classroom and how to integrate movement into the academic curriculum.

On touring this small town with a population under 3000, I was initially struck by the quiet beauty of the area and by the size and body habitus of the population. Everywhere I looked it seemed that people, children and adults were incredibly large with round, round faces and protuberant bellies hanging over their belts for those who could wear belts, but many were simply wearing pants with elasticized waist bands.

The next day at the school, a teacher remarked to me that most of the kids in her classroom were extremely overweight and depressed, unable to concentrate. She remarked that most of them got that way because in this community there was a high incidence of alcoholism, domestic and sexual violence. It had become almost a cultural custom: "Protect your kids from the predator (usually in your own home) by making them fat, ugly, hence unappealing. Fat boys and girls were not the ones who got raped, beaten or otherwise abused in this small community."

The school had specifically wanted workshops and teacher training for their staff that included dance in the hopes that dance, being a physical activity, would inspire the student population to get motivated to move (and that the creative aspect of the dance arts would inspire their souls). In his book, The Body Keeps the Score, *Bessel Van Der Kolk, M.D. describes that one avenue toward healing trauma is to let the body have experiences that deeply and viscerally contradict the helplessness, rage, or collapse that results from trauma.*

In her recently published book, Hunger A Memoir of (My) Body, NY Times bestselling author, Roxane Gay writes about how her path to morbid obesity, self-loathing, despair, desperation and depression was precipitated by a gang rape at the hands of a school mate and his friends. Like the youth of the rural town in Vermont, Gay writes "I was swallowing my secrets and making my body expand and explode. I found ways to hide in plain sight, to keep feeding a hunger that could never be satisfied—the hunger to stop hurting. I made myself bigger. I made myself safer."

Many years later I would come to learn that the trauma was often the common denominator lurking behind the twin symptoms of depression and obesity. I would also learn that sometimes the obesity came first and that mental and emotional collapse would follow years later as a person struggled throughout their lifetime within a culture that tends toward cruelty, intolerance and indifference towards people living with larger bodies.

Every day, across all medical specialties, physicians see people living with obesity. At the very least, I would encourage all of our colleagues to fine tune their listening skills when taking the history of their patient and to use available tools to assess for depression, anxiety, domestic violence regardless of why the patient has initially sought out the visit. When there are any signs of depression, mood disorder, or mental illness, refer the patient to an obesity medicine specialist whose four cornerstones of treatment are nutrition, physical activity, medication, and behavior. If the patient is in need of further support or treatment for psychosis, the obesity medicine specialist can also supply the appropriate referral to psychiatry. With the appropriate continuum of care, the result can be an engaged patient in a healing partnership.

Homework:

Are you eating your emotions? For the next two days, I want you to write down how the foods you are eating make you feel. Notice what foods come with positive emotions and notice what foods come with negative or darker emotions. Also notice your emotions and what foods you tend to reach for when you are feeling happy, sad, angry, tired, frustrated, anxious, awesome or excited.

Chapter 8

Purposeful Movement

FINDING YOUR SIGNATURE MOVEMENT: MOVEMENT IS MY MEDICINE

Movement IS my medicine, but WHY is movement my medicine? And perhaps why might you consider making movement your medicine?

Over the years with dance, performance, choreography, dance as education and therapy, yoga, qigong, dance as a two-way conduit to Spirit, dance as a part of Creative Aging, and now dance as a part of medicine, the influence of the arts is central to who I am as a human being. It is how I both process and share universal themes and concepts. What I know for sure is that if you want something to change in your life physically, emotionally, psychologically, or spiritually: MOVE! Shake it and your self up, quite literally.

Some of my earliest experiences with movement have to do with dance as spiritual expression. From a very early age I had the sense that I could speak to God through movement, but more importantly, God speaks to me when I dance and God speaks through me when I dance. I have been asked to dance in churches and holy places for most of my life.

Yoga saves my life too, and it can also save yours. Yoga becomes a pathway for connecting us to the deepest and truest parts of ourselves. It is a pathway to self-acceptance. It does that by teaching us to be aware of our breath. It also makes us aware of where our body is in space—where you begin and I end. This is important because spatial awareness tells us how to be around other people, and at the same time to find comfort and safety in the proximity.

Have you ever been in a class or other space where someone keeps bumping into you? You don't want to be that person. Yoga teaches us how to feel our edges from the inside out. Yoga is also important because it teaches self-acceptance and how to be appreciative of the body we have today.

When we gently connect with our bones, muscles, and fascia (the thin tissue that encases each muscle), we begin to know who we really are, deep down into our marrow and tissues, even down to the cellular level. So often, we get into mental and physical health problems because we ignore our bodies. Yoga is a user-friendly way to take charge of your physical, mental, and emotional health.

You can start this journey right now by taking two to three deep cleansing breaths: breathe in through your nose and out through your mouth with a soft sigh, "Ahhh." There it is: your "letting go" breath.

LAST DANCE

My father and I began studying qigong together in 2008, in what was to be his last year of life. We had been on a long journey with various cancers for 15 years. An athlete in his youth, he wanted to stay physically active, even while his physical strength was declining. I had just had foot surgery and weight bearing was not an option, so qigong was the perfect choice for father and daughter, as many postures and movements can be done from a seated position and some can even be done prone, while lying down.

I am grateful to my teachers for sharing the history and philosophy of qigong with me and my Dad. The beautiful yet powerful flowing motions of this practice are both movement and medicine. I will be practicing qigong for the rest of my life.

Just like my dad and I, kids and adults try learning this together!

BEGIN A QIGONG PRACTICE WITH OPENING AND THE THREE CORRECTIONS

1. Correcting the posture: Begin practice standing with the feet together. Step to the left, about shoulder width apart. Adjust your posture so that your body is upright and your spine is straight.

2. Correcting the breath: Deepen your breath, think 'soft belly.' Pay special attention to the exhalation breath and focus on your out breath. Let the breath out with a sigh or an "AHHHH" sound.

3. Correcting the mind: Direct your mind to a simple image such as clouds drifting across the sky.

MAKING A QI BALL

Making a Qi ball is about attuning our awareness, helping us to become aware of or find Qi in us. Begin by aligning your posture. The spaciousness of the sky and the solidity of the earth meet in you, creating a fertile ground for life changing energy in you. Deepen your breath and bring the palms together. Rub palms together, play with shaping or molding a ball. Notice the sensations in your hands.

Focus your mind: "Discovering Qi, I connect deeply with nature and become aware of a powerful new way of perceiving and being." (Jahnke 101-102)

DIRECT QI TO THE ORGANS

Rub your hands together and make heat to build up Qi. Place the right hand over the lower border of your rib cage, the location of the liver and the gallbladder. Place the left palm at the lower border of the rib cage, the location of the pancreas and the spleen. Be still and notice sensation, perhaps sending the energy from your organs to your hands and vice versa. Smile from the inside out. (Jahnke 138)

SEQUENCE 1:

1. OPENING PRACTICE WITH THE THREE INTENTIONAL CORRECTIONS

Focus your mind: "Purifying Qi I restore inner harmony by cleansing and dispelling spent, toxic, and unneeded Qi, and by opening to the inflow of fresh, natural life force and energy and power. "(Jahnke 130)

2. SPONTANEOUS QI

Spontaneous Qi (may also be spelled chi) is one of the most extraordinary of all qigong methods for many reasons. No method to learn it is spontaneous and intuitive. It is the best qigong method for dealing with shaking out or detoxifying Qi stagnation or emotional patterns that are trapped inside. This practice brings about coherence in the physiological and emotional aspects of the self. Historically, spontaneous qigong likely developed 40,000 to 60,000 years ago. Some ancient names are Primordial, Wuji Practice, Dancing Before Heaven, and Dancing in Chaos.

Align your posture, bend knees slightly and begin to bounce by lifting and dropping the heels. Do some variations on this activity. Shift your weight to the right so the right side is bouncing and the left is just along for the ride. Then bounce the left and let the right side just relax. Next add flopping your hands at the wrists or snapping your fingers. Wiggle the body and the limbs in any way that is comfortable. Allow the head and neck to move about, lift and drop your shoulders, even jump up and down. Do this for a few moments with deep, relaxed breathing.

Stop and turn your attention inward and feel the sensation. Ask yourself: "What do I feel and where do I feel it?" Sense your inner environment. Try a few movements with letting out an "Ahhh" or an "Ohhh" sound. Growl, laugh, shout or sigh, whatever sound brings the most relief right now…do it!

Think about shaking out all that no longer serves you. Think about shaking out tension and pain. Think about bringing in fresh Qi to replace that which is dispelled (Jahnke 91-93).

3. GATHER QI FROM EARTH AND HEAVEN

"This is a major key to all phases of Qi cultivation. You must gather, collect, absorb, and accumulate the Qi that is to be cultivated." Open your arms, bend your knees (back straight), gather from the earth (which is Yin) and bring the resource to your heart/mind. Open your arms and reach up to the Heavens (Yang); gather those resources and bring them down to the heart/mind. Begin again.

4. OPENING HEARTMIND

Step back on one leg with your arms and heart center open wide. Return and close arms in a self-hug. Step back with the other leg, arms open wide, return, close arms in a self-hug

5. STIR UP THE FIRE IN THE BELLY (DAN TIEN)

With open palms gently, lightly and quickly hit the area just below the naval in an upward fashion, alternating hands.

6. STEPPING UP

Move forward with strong energy. Move back.

7. PUSHING HANDS

Imagine that you are pushing away anything that does not serve you. Take your right hand and push across in front of the body to the left, change hands and push to the other side. Do this as many times as you wish until you create an imaginary empty space in front of you.

8. FILLING THE INNER COLUMN

Now fill in the space with whatever you need, washing down through the central channel through bones, marrow and organs. First sweep the right hand out to the side and then bring the hand and arm down through the central axis of the body.

Change hands, and do this as many times as feels right for you.

9. CLOSE PRACTICE

Embrace your tigers, your challenges. Step together, cross wrists, palms facing you, acknowledge your challenges, your tigers, embrace them and return to the mountaintop, which is you—your strength and rootedness. Return to the your mountain top as you push down to the space of the lower belly (your Dan Tien), the reservoir of your strength.

SEQUENCE 2

Here's a very short little qigong movement practice to remind us that we are designed to live long and healthy lives:

1. FLOWING MOTION

Slowly raise arms with palms up to the heart level. Turn palms down, lower arms. Breathe in as you go up, out as you go down. As you go up, raise up, slightly rolling over the balls of the feet. Roll back to a flat foot. As your arms pass slightly by your legs, curl your toes up a little. The Chinese say that if you do this 100 times a day, you will have good health. If you do this movement a 1000 time per day, you will live forever! Try this movement. You may even find that at first you need to hold on to something because the movement actually can help you improve balance!!

SEQUENCE 3

1. OPEN PRACTICE

3 corrections, incorporate making a Qi ball, directing Qi to the organs and spontaneous Qi

(See sequence 1)

2. WAITING AT THE TEMPLE GATE

Hands in prayer position by heart center, exhale as you swing arms down like a pendulum-eyes remain looking forward- inhale and bring hands over your head, then back to heart center.

3. CONSERVE QI, WATCHING CLOUDS:

"We can improve our inherent capacity or reservoir of Qi throughout our day by using mindfulness in decisions and behaviors that help to conserve Qi." Lift right arm with palm of hand facing your face. Left hand, fingers face forward positioned by the Dan Tien. Move both hands in the direction of the top elbow. The bottom hand sweeps across the belly to the right. The eyes follow the top hand. It is your cloud to watch! When you reach the right side, top hand floats down, bottom hand floats up so that you can follow the same motion to the left. Breath is full and deep. Repeat back and forth.

4. PURIFY QI

This can build connective tissue, strengthen and help protect against disease. Start with hand level with heart. Breathe in, face palms out, exhale as you push out to the sides with tension. Breathe in, relax as you bring arms back to the heart level. In the same manner, push above (exhale push with tension, inhale, relax, return to heart center), then in front of you, then down. Keep your torso erect rather than bending over so that the Qi flows.

5. CIRCULATE QI

"Qi will increase its circulation spontaneously as soon as we have removed the first and most disastrous block-constant, insidious, low grade internal tension." Palms face each other at heart level. Turn to your right, press palms forward as you exhale and shift weight gently pushing forward. This clears the space for fresh Qi. Turn palms to face you as you inhale and move fresh Qi back toward your HeartMind. Turn palms down to circulate Qi down along your front leg as you breathe out. Weight remains on the back leg. Gather Qi from the earth as you breathe in and draw it back up the leg channels. Gently turn to the other side to circulate Qi in the same manner.

6. RING THE TEMPLE GONG

Twist at the waist, let your arms go along for the ride, look behind over your shoulder, let your hands or soft fists tap your body to stimulate and ring Qi to kidneys in the back, liver and gall bladder on the right and spleen and pancreas on the left. Breathe fully.

7. CLOSE PRACTICE

*Embrace Tiger and Return to the Mountaintop (See Step 9 in sequence 1).

RESOURCES FOR QIGONG

The Healing Promise of Qi: Creating Extraordinary Wellness Through QiGong and Tai Chi, Roger Jahnke, O.M.D. (2002)

More Energy More Life: The Lift Chi Up, Pour Chi Down Method, Master Mingtong Gu (2013)

Spirit of the Dancing Warrior: Asian Wisdom for Peak Performances in Athletics and Life, Jerry Lynch and Chungliang Al Huang (2010)

QiGong Homework for Kids, Parents, Guardians: Okay the idea here is to have fun, explore and move! You can try picking one or two moves, or try to do an entire sequence. Explore, don't worry about getting it right. Instead, keep noticing how you feel when you move.

Try this: Notice a time when you are feeling heavy or down, sad or angry, then try some of these movements and literally see if you can 'move' the heavy, sad, tired, down feeling up and out of your body. Pay attention to your emotions and feelings before and after you move.

I have written the next two stories to provide another perspective on movement and its value. The first story is for the adults to enjoy, and I hope it is a story that will inspire as well. I want to remind all the parents and guardians (especially the women) who are reading this book that their dreams and aspirations are important and that when we have dreams it helps our kids have dreams of their own.

Dancing, Doctoring, Determination and Other Acts of Quiet Resistance/Revolution

People often ask me about the relationship between dancing and doctoring. The art of dance is my bridge builder; it is how I explain the world and the universe to myself. It is the way I make this internal dialogue visible. Movement is a metaphor for all of life, and something I know for sure is that I would have no life without movement. Choreographing and directing a women's dance company is another way extending this expression out into the world. It is also a quiet and persistent act of resistance and revolt for me, against boundaries, against others trying to define me and put me into a category of what fits their definition of what it means to be a woman, a wife, a mother, a doctor, or even a dancer for that matter.

The women and I that make up Core of Fire are as much a Community of Resistance and revolution as we are a gathering of women who collectively desire to express ourselves through dance and movement, saying no to aging in graceless, bodies that have become undesirable even to ourselves. We say an equal yet opposite no as well to being objectified and choose instead to define ourselves to ourselves for ourselves. We often commune with our immortal ancestors, moving forward in the world while shape shifting perceptions of how women are supposed to move in the world; how and when we can be seen in the world. We dare to shapeshift ourselves, putting on colors and costumes to illustrate our mood and our emotions. We color our lips, tint our cheeks, and darken our eyelashes, so when our gaze meets yours, there is no mistaking the truth we speak with our stare; the honor we bring; the life givers and signifiers that we are today and everyday.

These are acts of resistance/revolution because 50, 60, and 70 something professionals with degrees and desk jobs, husbands, and children are supposed to be settling into a middle-aged colorless purgatory, defined and confined by others expectations. No thank you we say, collectively and individually. No thank you, I say for movement is both my life and my medicine and you may take neither for granted.

Kids, here is my dance story for you. Hopefully it will inspire and encourage you.

Healing Dance

On Sunday, July 20, Core of Fire was invited to participate in a summer service led by Rev. Zemoria Brandon, entitled "The Sparkle of the Diamond Depends on its Flaws." Our first offering was a danced processional piece entitled, "Walking Forward." Here, the dancers move down the aisle in dignity and majesty, processing toward a row of thrones suggesting that as the beloved body gathers in community, they too are coming to sit upon the throne of their being, coming home to their true selves.

I truly believe that dance or as my dear friend Rev. Zemoria refers to it, sacred dance, is a healing modality. Unique because it is so primal, taking us to a place beyond words and before language. Each person sharing sacred movement and as each person watching sacred movement becomes in their own way danced and healed by Spirit.

After this particular service, a man approached me to share what occurred for him when watching "Walking Forward." There is a gesture in the dance where the dancers extend their right arm forward, index finger in the air, feet planted. As the singer sings "never looking back," we turn our torsos with arm extended, finger pointing heavenward, 180 degrees, and then back again. This gesture is repeated several times. The man went on to say that the strength he saw in our hands took him back to a story he learned in childhood about how humans came to have the philtrum below our nose, contiguous with the center of our upper lips. The story from the Jewish tradition goes something like this: With every conception comes an angel, and that angel tells every unborn child the history of the world and of life, the secrets of life and love. Just as the child enters its mother's birth canal, its angel taps it just below the nose, causing the indentation and causing the child to forget. After we are born, it becomes our job to remember. The man looked at me and smiled and said, "Thank you, for I have remembered some very important pieces of my life sitting here today."

Perhaps to help with your own remembering and healing, try the following: Take a slow purposeful mindful walk. Pick a spot that is peaceful to you or perhaps a favorite place, not too far from home or even the block where you live. Go on a walking quest, quiet your mind by paying attention to your surroundings, really see the sidewalk, the sand, the tree, the path or wherever you are walking. Perhaps ever so often, pause, close your eyes, and ask yourself, 1) How am I moving forward in my life? 2) What deep wisdom am I remembering when I allow myself to become quiet? 3) Consider using this quiet walking time to explore some ideas about what you might like to do when you grow up. Share your thoughts, ideas with parents/guardians, the adults that you trust and value most in your life.

Dance As Prayer

The next two dance stories features the idea of dance as prayer or sacred movement. I bet some of you already dance your prayers or feel connected to the spiritual when you hear certain music and move in certain ways. The first dance called "Be Still and Know" is meant to be performed by two dancers.

Dance has always been a sacred practice for me. For as long as I can remember and probably even before that, dance has not only been the way I speak to God, but when I move, dance is the way that God speaks to me and through me.

"I am life, and life is the only truth. Every animal, every flower, every rock is life, because everything is full of life. All of us are only one living being, and we come from the same place."
–Author Unknown

"Be Still and Know": The two dancers sit, appearing human but only embodied in their human form, hovering between the worlds of heaven and earth. Completely still, on a slight diagonal, angled toward each other. An entire stanza of music is sung before any movement occurs. The dance is simple, sparse, ideally the feet of the dancers do not move until the third movement or third stanza of the song. The power of the dance is rooted in the grounding of the feet, the depth and intention of the breath, the simple reaches and rises and falls; all done in call and response. At one moment there is the impulse for the dancers to face each other and when they do, there is that spark of divine connection as surely we are gazing into the eyes of the Beloved and there is no other, only the true self and love.

Yes, be still and know. The patterned call and response hand movements—who leads, who follows? The turning outward on the final stanza and inviting in the viewer, inviting what may have seemed on the outside to come in, where all become one and there truly is no other. And finally, at the end, the embrace, the hug, the dancers settle more fully into their human form, renewed in spirit, born again, if you will in that moment, stepping back into the earthly world hand-in-hand to walk amongst us once again.

"At the still point of the turning world.

Neither flesh nor fleshless;

Neither from nor towards; at the still point,

There the dance is,

but neither arrest nor movement. And do not call it fixity,

Where past and future are gathered. Neither movement from nor towards,

Neither ascent nor decline. Except for the point, the still point,

There would be no dance, and there is only

The dance."

T.S. Eliot, Four Quartets (1943)

Your Homework:
Kids and Parents/Guardians give yourself the gift of being still and knowing, sitting quietly if only for a few moments each day. Maybe even play a favorite piece of music and if you like move a bit to the music. Try it with a quiet piece of music and try it with a piece of music that makes you want to dance all over. Notice how you feel with each. I recommend doing this at the beginning of your day, really think of serving yourself a generous portion of meditation as part of your breakfast and part of what nourishes you for the day. You will find that on the days that you make the time to sit quietly, you will be providing much needed nourishment to your nervous system, your metabolism, as well your gut-brain axis (to mention a few of the benefits). At the end of the day, if you are able to give yourself a 'happy hour' that includes a nourishing meal, a few minutes of sitting in quiet, noticing and deeply listening within and without, the day's tensions melt away and your awareness and breath transforms you into a being that is able to let go, and allow the brain to turn towards the work of preparing one for sleep, recharging and dream time. When you wake up the next morning, what do you remember, what do you notice? To really anchor in the benefits of this practice this week, keep a notepad or a journal at bedside and write what comes.

Next here's a dance story that highlights movement from everyday life. Often used as both a theater technique and a dance technique, this style of movement, sometimes called improvisation, can be a very effective way to tell a story.

"ALL THIS JOY":
The dancers are moving, at first all seemingly in separate worlds. Someone appears to be reading a book, another gardening, someone having cocktails, someone else hanging up clothes. The audience watches, drawn in, recognizing the common everyday movements they themselves do. A dancer looks up from her everyday movement and reaches to another dancer, extending her hand in a gesture of connection, that dancer then reaches to another and then that one reaches to another until a circle of light, life, and love forms with the dancers facing inward. Breath, the eyes look up, breath the eyes are cast down, breath the eyes lift up and meet the gaze of another across the circle. Then the dancers begin to move first in one direction and then in the other direction, walking deliberately, feet firmly planted with each step, again drawing the audience in both visually and emotionally, hands reaching high arms coming down in an embrace felt by all in the circle and all who witness the circle. In that moment, people watching become a part of the dance feeling embraced and held themselves. There is often an audible silence that sends this moment in the dance to a soul place that invites healing and reflection for the viewer.

The dance continues incorporating American Sign Language to express the message of Life, Spirit, Love. The dancers break apart in pairs, twirling and laughing, embracing and comforting each other as both all the joy and all the pain of life is expressed in the inspirational and beautiful music of John Denver. Finally, the music quiets and the dancers become individuals again, each back in her own world, leaving the audience to reflect, many often in tears, perhaps remembering all the joy and all the pain in this time on earth we call life.

This dance, choreographed 11 years ago by me and first performed a few days before Thanksgiving in 2007, has become my most frequently requested piece.

Yes, sometimes we humans must meet in a place that is beyond words, in a place that lies beyond the reaches of our frontal lobes to think, judge, and make up stories about our past and predictions about our future. Sometimes we need something that allows us to drop into the space of just being ourselves without pretense, that carries us beyond shame, embarrassment, and limitation and into a knowingness and openness that teleports us to God, if only for the briefest of moments. This dance seems to do just that, all this joy, all this sorrow.

Homework:

Draw yourself as your favorite dance or movement, or draw your relationship to movement.

Chapter 9

The Power of Intentions and Affirmations

An intention is what one intends to accomplish or attain. Intentions can be very useful when we are trying to organize our day or reach a goal or objective.

Does your intention have an intention?

So often we set forth into our day at work or school with the greatest of intentions. Today I am calm. Today I am patient. At the end of the day, we often feel disappointed, shortchanged, and we are left wondering what happened. Does this sound at all familiar?

If it does, what is missing is the practice of being intentional about our intentions. The practice of being mindful needs to be carried out through the day; it's a journey and a process. Kids, think of it this way. Ever go to your doctor and the doctor tells you to take your medication two times per day, once in the morning with your breakfast and once at night with your dinner? Just like we take some medications or supplements in divided doses to maximize their effectiveness, we also need to do this with our intentions. Over time we can reduce the practice to once a day dosing!

Try the following tips to help your intention have an intention:

- Set the stage of your mind. Take a few minutes to prepare your mind and tap into your subconscious by taking a few deep breaths, even 1-3 minutes of focusing on your breath to create a state of relaxed awareness. Now you are ready to listen, inwardly, to your self.
- What are you hoping to get out of this day? When you brush your teeth tonight and look into the mirror, what will you be saying to yourself? Set your intention first thing in the morning after you have completed Step 1. It may be something like this: At the end of the day, I would like to feel at ease and at peace. Or it may be stated in another way: Today my intention is to move through my day with ease and peace, not letting anyone ruffle my feathers or upset me. I will come back to my breath in those moments and focus on keeping my peace in all situations.
- When stuff comes up and you find yourself reacting (and you know, stuff comes up all the time), your default button will be to return to your breath, to be intentional about your intention. Repeat step two as often as necessary throughout your day.
- Please don't be afraid to set a reminder or alarm on your phone or other device such as a watch, any of your handheld devices, or even your computer at work or school. These little mini breaks of being intentional

will also allow you to clear your mind and be more effective at performing the task at hand.

Homework:

Each day this week try creating an intention for your day. For instance, by the end of today I want to have started or completed these three things: ______, _______, _______, and at the end of the day I want to feel happy, relaxed, and grateful. Create an intention for each day of the week.

USING AFFIRMATIONS

An affirmation is a positive statement that we create for the purpose of self-encouragement or direction. Affirmations can be used to help us get back on track and they remind us to speak nicely and with kindness even to ourselves. Below are some affirmations I use to give myself an emotional tune-up and to remind myself of how much God loves me. God loves you too. Feel free to borrow any of these any time you need a boost:

- Remember always that God is Love.
- Love really is all there is.
- Joy dwells in the soul; it's your birthright.
- Prosperity begins with your state of mind.
- My prosperity begins with my state of mind.
- Abundance: look at a beach and think about counting the grains of sand; we live in an endlessly abundant universe.
- The path to true freedom begins with knowing one's own mind.
- Unity is understanding inner unity within yourself, notice your breath as you breathe in and out; sleeping and awake; eyes open and closed; balanced, we are living unity.
- Harmony is a state of mind; it's an inside job.
- Creativity: We are all naturally creative for we are

made in the image and likeness of creativity itself.

- Purpose: We all have a unique purpose, make the time to know and understand what your purpose is and then become and do what is yours to do.
- AllOne: We are all on a voyage home, we are all one with creative mind.
- True intimacy is a life sustaining gift that is quite literally as close as our fingertips.
- Life is a true adventure, requiring bravery and courage.
- The Peace that passes all understanding is that still small voice that whispers in the ear of your soul every day; listen and hear yourself.
- Growth: We have many yardsticks in life by which to measure our real growth be on the lookout for yours.
- The Truth not only sets you free, it lets you your soul soar and inspires and uplifts all those around you.
- Remember who you really are.
- Live your life so as to regret nothing.
- Light your path with your Truth, spoken with love and compassion.
- Union with God is the only relationship worth pursuing; get this and get everything.

- Just as the ocean refuses no river; your soul refuses no part of your life; allow yourself to flow home to yourself.
- Night Flight: our dreams can take us to magic mountains and hidden valleys of the spirit where deep healing occurs.
- Landing is the treasure chest at journey's end.

Homework:
Kids, parents/guardians try creating your own week's worth of affirmations. Write one positive affirmation every day for seven days. The following week, read all seven aloud every morning for seven days. At each day's end, notice the difference in your day.

Chapter 10

The Power of Mindset and Mindset Shifts and Holds

Mindset involves setting our mind up to be our best friend. It means we have learned how to keep the negative self-talk at bay, and we now have powerful anecdotes for it. Oftentimes the anecdotes are a type of affirmation that begins with the words "I am." Here are 49 "I am" affirmations to say to yourself whenever you are feeling a bit blue or a bit down or if someone tries to put you down or bully you.

1. I am beautiful.
2. I am loved beyond measure.
3. I am powerful.
4. The intelligence of the Universe lives inside of me.
5. I am creative.
6. I am smart.
7. I am uniquely me and there is no one else exactly like me.

8. I love and take great care of myself.
9. I am able to forgive myself and forgive others.
10. I honor my body by getting enough sleep and rest.
11. I honor my body by nourishing myself with healthy water and nutritious foods.
12. I can do anything I set my mind on.
13. I am filled with goodness and light.
14. I treat myself with love, kindness, and respect.
15. I am healthy and getting stronger every day.
16. I am an amazing problem solver.
17. I value education both in and out of school.
18. I am an amazing learner.
19. I learn well and easily.
20. I express my gratitude and appreciation for all of life.
21. I am grateful for the little things.
22. I am able to forgive myself and others.
23. I have an open and loving heart.
24. I am wise.
25. I am compassionate.
26. I have everything I need right now.

27. I value and treasure my emotions and feelings.
28. I am a great contributor to my household.
29. I love and honor my parents/guardian(s).
30. I am inspired, excited and enthusiastic.
31. I love my culture and ancestors.
32. I am ready and up to the challenges of life.
33. I am an overcomer.
34. I am amazing!
35. I am here on earth to do great things.
36. I am royalty!
37. I am curious, willing and able to learn new ideas.
38. I am a great leader.
39. I am able to study and practice happiness.
40. I am joyful.
41. I am capable and know that the world is a better place because of me.
42. I am both a giver and receiver.
43. I am able to see all sides of a situation and welcome different points of view.
44. I am able to tap into my creative potential everyday.
45. I am able to value my dreams and the messages they bring.

46. I am able to speak my truth with compassion.
47. I am fully alive in my body and move with grace and ease.
48. I am able to transform my setbacks into my comebacks.
49. I am a loving presence who loves God.
50. I am good enough right now.
51. I am enough.
52. I am perfectly made to fulfill my unique purpose in life.
53. I am continuously learning and growing.

Homework: Kids/ Parents/Guardians,
Read seven I am" affirmations in the morning or evening for each day of the week. Challenge yourself and write your own.

For each change we make in life, we also need to create a different mindset shift and a mindset hold. The mindset shift is kind of like our bridge. As we make our change and go across the bridge from point a to point b, we must also remember to take our minds with us and let our new thoughts, ideas, flourish and take root. Creating our new mindset shift can be a tricky step, because this is when our current 'mind' set can keep us stuck in old ways and habits that don't allow us to fully move forward.

Another way of thinking of mindset shifts is to think of it as the time we can create new habits to go along with our new idea, project or goal. Our mindset shift period is usually minimally a period of 21 days for the new habit to form. Once the mindset shift period is over, we are ready for the next step and that is the step of owning the new you or the new situation and that can be thought of as your mind set hold. A good question to ask ourselves is "what will it take for me to sustain the new me, from being a better student and getting better grades in school, or (for the adults) to improving job performance and succeeding to a greater degree in the workplace.

I also believe that if we want a better, safer world where we all can thrive, kids and adults alike, we are going to have to get pretty good at establishing mindset, establishing new habits with our mindset shifts and then developing our mindset holds to allow us to fully own the change and become the change we actually want to see in the world. Everything we have been exploring and talking about is something that we can all participate in to find our way to a state of relaxed awareness. It is from this place of relaxed awareness that we can create anything we want because we are able to be clear minded and clear thinking. This is true if we are 10, 20, 40, or 80. Hopefully everyone who is reading this understands that besides needing to sleep and eat well (and this also includes stay well hydrated), we need to include in our life on a daily basis at least one of the practices discussed in this book: meditation, guided imagery, yoga, qigong, prayer, and spiritual development.

End Notes

Well for now dear readers—kids, parents, and guardians alike—we have come to the end of our journey. I want you to use these practices, tools, and techniques to find strength and joy in your lives and to make our world a better place. I am leaving you with something to consider and three requests that I believe could be your next steps forward in making this world a safe, thriving, global community for all: Truth Telling, Salvaging, and Choosing our Guides.

1. Truth telling: We must learn to speak our truth with compassion. Our very lives are at stake. The pendulum of balance must swing back towards peace, hope, and charity for all. Learn how to speak up and out with wisdom, passion, and intelligence. The world needs the clarity of your voice, whether you are 12 or 112.

2. Salvaging: We have dominion over this Earth and all she is connected to in the known and unknown Universe. The conversations about sustainability were good ones, but those days are now bygone if we are to remain here as a species. We must put our heads together across the generations and create a revolution of regeneration and renewal. We are going to need mathematicians, scientists,

physicians, environmentalists, engineers, educators and global thought leaders to heal the earth and make our planet safe for humans now and in the future.

3. Choosing our Guides: We must walk with Wisdom through this uncharted territory. For those with eyes to see and ears to hear, you are amongst the chosen to rise up and walk forward with Love and Righteousness on either side to bring humanity back home to center.

Hurry now to the nearest mirror, for the global leaders that we need today are looking right back at you now, no matter your age! We all need to thrive as we come together to meditate in a time of madness and we change the world together, kids, parents and guardians—one meditation at a time.

"Grace and peace be yours in abundance." 2 Pet. 1:2

Acknowledgments

This book would not have been written without the presence, support, and influence of several key people. My family and an omnipresent and loving Universal Spirit, God that infuses light and life every day through my mother, Alma, my husband and life partner in all things, Diem Jones, my sons, Keita, and Dima. A special offering of gratitude to Keita, who insisted that my thoughts be put to paper in the form of a book. Keita, it finally happened! My coach and mentor, Dr. Draion Burch, who has become the wind beneath the wings of so many dreams and who has shared so unselfishly his gifts and talents so I could walk in my purpose. My other coaches, Dr. Taunya Lowe, the Empress of Mindset Mastery and Dr. Bonnie Simpson for teaching the fine art of Due Diligence and Contract Negotiations but really teaching me that I am worth the time it takes to be thorough in all matters as it relates to me and mine and to be a good steward, because I am worthy. To my minister, Angela Denton and my communities of faith. The beautiful women who keep my soul together by dancing with me every week for the past 12 years, Core of Fire. Gratitude also goes to a new group of women in my life who first heard the whisperings of this book in July 2018, in Broward County, Florida and who listened so intently and with such ferocity that the first words were born and found their way to the page. To my Lion Queens, I hear you ROAR. Thank you for hearing my whisper. Special thank you to Dr. James Gordon, my Center for Mind Body Medicine family, and Rowan University School of Osteopathic Medicine.

About the Author

Dr. Carol Penn, DO, MA, FACCE, Dipl. ABOM, is doubly board-certified in family medicine and obesity medicine. A master Mindset, Meditation, and Movement Coach, she is the Director of Service Integration for Ocean Health Initiatives, a federally qualified healthcare center in New Jersey. Dr. Penn is also CEO and founder of Penn Global Visions, LLC, and lead consultant of All ONE Consulting Group, LLC, of New Jersey; medical correspondent for WURD Radio Station in Philadelphia; certified health, wellness, and fitness coach; founder and artistic director of Core of Fire Interfaith Dance Ministry, and more.

Prior to becoming a physician, Dr. Carol danced with the Alvin Ailey American Dance Theater Company and School. In addition, she has served as a teaching fellow and consultant to the Kennedy Center for the Performing Arts, as well as tenured fine arts faculty of the DC Public Schools. Dr. Carol has toured internationally as a dancer and speaker.

Reach her online @drcarolpenn,
drcarol@drcarolpenn.com, or www.drcarolpenn.com

CPSIA information can be obtained
at www.ICGtesting.com
Printed in the USA
JSHW051002080822
28826JS00001BA/5